THE WAY TO LIFE

BENJAMIN HOFF

The Way to Life

At the Heart of the Tao Te Ching

New York · WEATHERHILL · *Tokyo*

A NOTE ON THE TITLE-PAGE DECORATION. The Chinese ideograph meaning "path" or "way" is the first word of the *Tao Te Ching*.

First edition, 1981

Published by John Weatherhill, Inc., of New York and Tokyo, with editorial offices at 7-6-13 Roppongi, Minato-ku, Tokyo 106, Japan. Printed and first published in Japan.

Library of Congress Cataloging in Publication Data: Hoff, Benjamin, 1946– / The way to life. / Includes English translations of selections from the Tao te ching. / 1. Lao-tzu. Tao te ching. / I. Lao-tzu. Tao te ching. English. Selections. 1980. / II. Title. / BL1900. L35H645 / 299'.51482 / 80–18309 / ISBN 0–8348–0156–6

CONTENTS

AROUND 2,500 years ago, a man appeared at Han-ku Pass in northwest China, traveling toward the wilderness beyond the border. The Keeper of the Pass recognized the man known as Lao-tze, Old Master, and realized from his words that he did not intend to return. He begged Lao-tze to leave some of his guiding principles. After many refusals, Lao-tze gave in and wrote what he considered to be useful on some bamboo tablets. He presented these and resumed his journey, vanishing from sight.

The statements he left behind have come to be known as the *Tao Te Ching* (Tao Virtue Classic), the book of Tao and its characteristics. Tao can roughly be described as the ways or laws of the life force found within all things at all times as well as the inner power itself, inseparable from its external actions. Literally, Tao means road, path, or way; following Tao can mean working with universal energy and its natural laws.

Lao-tze was an older contemporary of K'ung Fu-tze (Confucius). Both emphasized the need for social harmony through positive moral behavior on the part of citizens, and honest, conscientious government on the part of rulers. But to Lao-tze, responsible action and moral living depended more upon inner development and individual conscience than upon conformity to group patterns of the moment. He maintained that a sound citizen, without feeling forced to follow predetermined rules of conduct, and without being conditioned to wait for the artificial incentive of external reward, would naturally do what he could to help others, not even having to think about it. In contrast, K'ung Fu-tze tended to emphasize obligations and see good deeds as tools for building social merit. Unlike K'ung Fu-tze, Lao-tze believed that prevailing educational methods and values placed oppressive obstacles in the way of personal happiness and healthy social relations. While K'ung Fu-tze gave elaborate advice to those in high positions of power, Lao-tze urged rulers to govern by simply serving with detachment, compassion, and humility, and warned what will happen when a government loses touch with the governed through issuing excessive demands and relying upon retaliatory rules and regulations. He cautioned against cruel and arrogant military leadership, recommending that those in command conduct their victories like funerals.

Beyond their common goal of individual and political harmony, Taoists and Confucianists differed greatly in attitude and approach. Confucian conduct was characteristically rigid and rational; that of Taoism, essentially fluid and mystical. Confucianism concerned itself with the complexities of communal hierarchy—how much honor to give to whom, under what circumstances. Taoism advised treating others as equals, neither looking down upon nor envying anyone. The Confucianist's outlook was guided by *jen,* fellowship or benevolence, measured out to others through making intellectual distinctions on various levels. The Taoist used *tz'u,* unlimited love or compassion. Confucianists created complicated methods of classifying members of a society as superior or inferior. Taoists criticized the coldness of such systems which they said succeeded mostly in increasing the distance between the ones labeled superior and those who needed their help, and suggested a simpler way of determining true superiority without encouraging snobbishness: the superior man was one who cared, and the inferior man was one who did not. Confucian ethics made use of many rules, stories, and sayings. Taoism generally avoided them, relying instead upon personal experience and intuition. The *Tao Te Ching,* the major written presentation of Taoism, is a masterpiece of brevity; it begins and ends by warning of the limitations and weaknesses of words. Instead of an involved, intellectual explanation of the power of Tao, Lao-tze used the image of the river, pointing out that the gentlest force will overcome the most resisting force, as the softest water will shape the hardest stone.

Over the last few centuries, the eighty-one quiet chapters of the *Tao Te Ching* have been translated countless times into one language after another, sending their homespun analogies to the farthest foreign lands on earth. In China, their solitary simplicity has been used to sanctify the existence of the ornate religious cult of popular Taoism with its gaudy gallery of demons and ghosts. This has succeeded mostly in remarkably distorting and ignoring the meanings of Lao-tze's teachings, taking the most superstitious rituals and beliefs from other religions, and using the name of Taoism to mislead the ignorant for financial gain. Anti-intellectual, indifferent to the abstract mental world of philosophy, the *Tao Te Ching* has been claimed by intellectuals and philosophers everywhere, and is often filed under Philosophy in bookstores. Its unpretentious yet profound passages attract meddlesome scholars of minute definition, many of whom seem more concerned with being technically safe, and with quarreling among themselves, than with aiding the awareness of others by presenting clear, coherent interpretations of the communications contained within its pages. The direct, concise spirit of Lao-tze's writing is often overlooked. The pedantic writer is easily lost in uncertainty over the meanings of many obsolete characters in the earliest surviving copies of the *Tao Te Ching,* and easily lost in confusion over the comments mixed in with them by others; the reader is then easily lost in meaningless messages and indecisive writing. But when the reader is lost, the Way is lost. Even if analytical exactness were possible in interpreting the many meanings of all the ancient characters, it would not be sufficient or appropriate—experiencing and describing the Way go beyond such matters.

The *Tao Te Ching* has sometimes also suffered from the weakening words of those who attempt to shape its universal truth into expressions of individual ego. As in the previous approach, when the soothing waters of its essential simplicity are stirred up by excessive and misused words, its crystal clarity turns cloudy, and the *Tao Te Ching* becomes mysterious and obscure. Both extremes, unimaginative examination and undisciplined display of surface skill, miss the unity of the Way through incompleteness and imbalance. Such one-sided efforts are in vain; the Tao cannot be measured, contained, or forced. It passes through limitations as the river slips through the fingers, flowing to where the egotistical or merely intellectual mind cannot follow.

Regardless of the interpretation of obsolete characters, the timeless message of the *Tao Te Ching* is: work with the universal natural laws. When you follow the patterns reflected in the everyday operations of the natural world and stop struggling for what your childish, interfering ego demands that you do for it, whatever you deserve will be attracted to you, whenever it is most needed. Moving in cooperation with the currents of Tao, you will easily arrive at wherever it is best for you to be at the moment. Fighting against them, you will sooner or later lose control. Those who master the skills of sailing learn this, as do those who master their own lives. The same principles are effective everywhere.

The individual in harmony with the teachings of the *Tao Te Ching,* while spiritually a conscious, integral part of the universe, is emotionally independent. He may have many friends and be surrounded by a vast society, but he recognizes that he was born alone and will die alone. He passes through life with eyes of his own, seeing what others cannot see. He does not expect anyone else to be able to see through his eyes, as he knows that such unnatural expectations only lead to disappointment, loneliness, and sorrow. The escapist, who cannot face the fact that he also is an individual, hides in a crowd, wanders in dreams, runs from the world. The Taoist walks the other way. The real world is his place of business, more meaningful to him than the pursuit of exhausting obsessions or the worship of idle dreams. Free from the confinement of the infantile ego and the chains of unnecessary possessions, he grows and works effortlessly with Tao. Though obscured by persuasive illusions and temporary pleasures, the Tao continuously creates and sustains, giving serenity, lasting happiness, and strength.

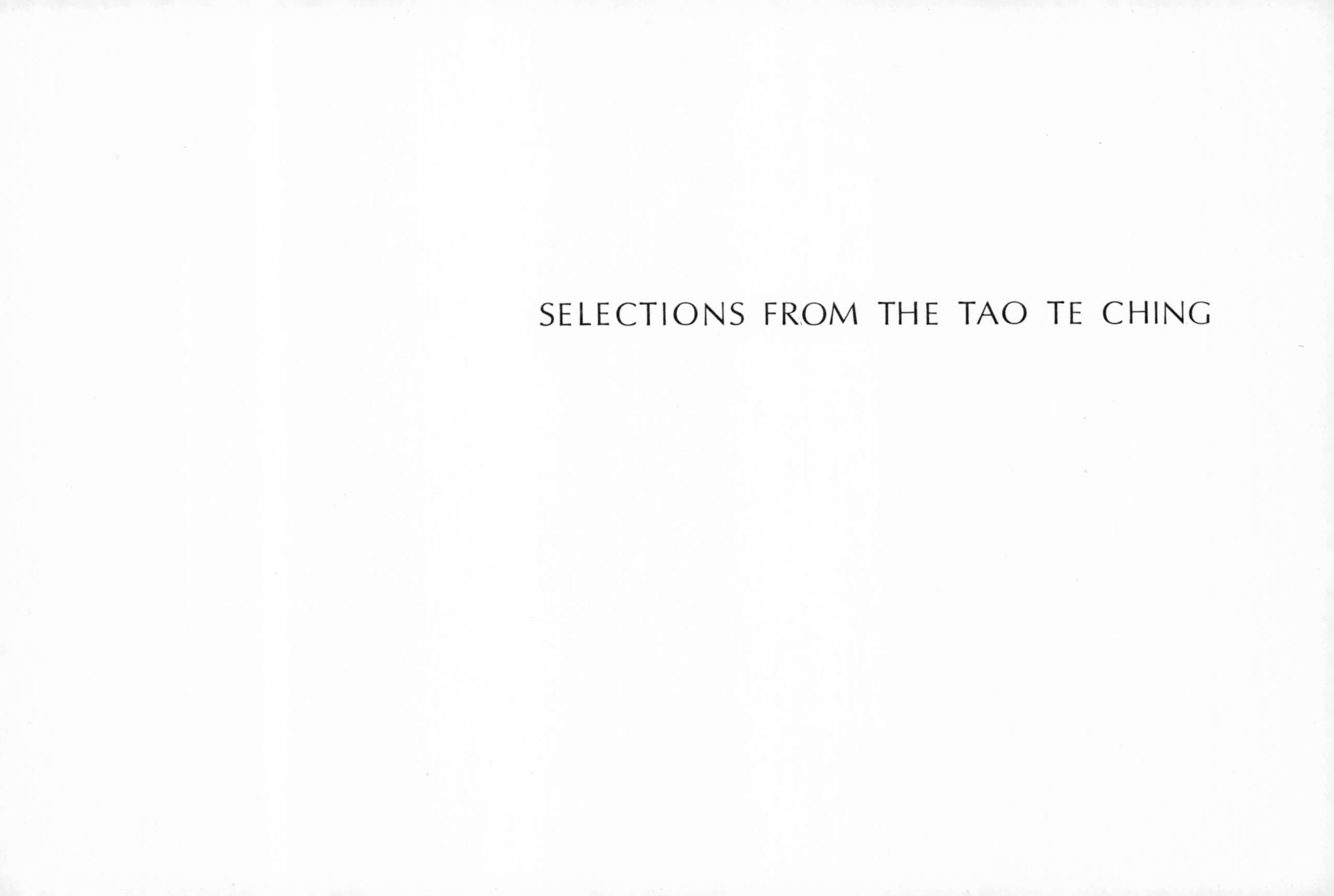

SELECTIONS FROM THE TAO TE CHING

THE WAY that can be defined to death is not the Way to Life.
The road that can be measured is not the endless road.
From nothing, the infinite universe began.
From no number, its countless things appeared.
From no name, their limitless source will be known.

Looking out, its effects are seen;
Looking in, their cause is discovered.
With words, these are considered separate;
With vision, they are recognized as one.

TO HEAVEN,
The ten thousand things
Are ceremonial straw figures,
Each made for a purpose,
Honored,
Then thrown away.

To the wise,
The people seem the same.
Being born,
Living,
Dying,
All appear,

Perform their parts,
Then vanish.

In either case,
The Tao within is not what is created,
The Tao within is not what is destroyed.
Unborn,
Undying,
It gives life to heaven and earth.

As things of straw stand for those behind them,
So things of the world represent the Way.

THE GATEWAY to the highest understanding
Will be found in the lowest valley.
From its stillness,
The most enduring actions will be born.
Within its mystery,
The clearest answers will arise.
Although it may appear empty,
It will never be exhausted.

The Spirit of the Valley
Creates life without end.

SENSATIONALISM will wear you down.

The five colors blind the eye.
The five sounds deafen the ear.
The five flavors deaden the appetite.
Chasing and killing destroy the heart.
Precious possessions cripple one's mastery;
They end up owning their owners.

The wise are guided by what they know to be true,
Not manipulated by what they are told.
This is common sense.
Using common sense,
They refuse to be misled.
Refusing to be misled,
They avoid being trapped.

HEAVEN and earth are ageless.
They constantly change,
They grow,
They escape confining limitations.
Following their example,
The wise go beyond themselves.
Receding,
They are advanced.
Being detached from their own images,
They are united with all.
Forgetting fame,
They are remembered.

WATER effortlessly nourishes ten thousand things.
It flows to places that the proud and analytical ignore.
It is like the Tao.

As the rivers run,
Those of Tao concern themselves
With what is useful and efficient.
Their thoughts are strong and deep,
Their relations flexible,
Their words reflect the truth.
Their power is balanced and beneficial,
Their skills acquired through experience,
Their actions well timed.
Wherever they are,
They are at home.

Rocks are hard and unyielding;
The rivers flow around them and forget.

THE TEN thousand things have their beginning
In absolute emptiness,
Complete quiet.
Energetically growing,
Restlessly changing,
All complete themselves
By returning to stillness.

The wise see the action and its foundation;
The foolish see only the changes.

From a quiet mind comes vision;
From vision comes knowledge of unity;
From knowledge of unity comes compassion for all.
From compassion comes greatness,
From greatness comes Tao.

From Tao comes life without end.

When deceit begins,
Honesty is discovered.
When weakness develops,
Strength is recognized.
When arrogance increases,
Respect is appreciated.
When cruelty becomes common,
Kindness is admired.
When treachery is everywhere,
Loyalty is rewarded.

A nation of heroes
Is a nation in trouble.

WOOD forms the wheel's hub;
The space within makes it useful.
Clay shapes the pitcher;
The space within makes it useful.
Walls define the room;
Windows, doors, and the space within make it
useful.
Appearance comes from what is there;
Value comes from what is not.

Filled with ego is not the Way.

DISGRACE or honor—which is worse?

Since both upset the balance of the world,
The wise see both as unnatural.
They know that whatever is raised too high
Will later fall;
That whatever is held down against its nature
Will later rise without restraint.
Honor brings conceit,
Conceit causes mistakes,
Mistakes lead to disgrace.
Being unconcerned with honor and disgrace,
You will bring no misfortune upon yourself.

When you see the world as part of yourself,
You will take care of it.
When you see yourself as part of the world,
You will be taken care of.

FROM ancient times,
The masters of life have been silent and sensible,
Separate and serene.
Although we cannot see their inner power,
We can observe its effect;
We can describe their appearance.

They watch, like men who know danger,
Constantly alert, as when crossing a stream in the middle of winter,
Considerate as visiting guests.
They yield, resembling melting ice;
They become simple, appearing as uncarved blocks of wood;
They recede, like deep water in dark caves.

If a man cannot wait, he cannot know the right time to move.
If he cannot be still, his actions will have gathered no power.

Stir muddy water, and it will stay cloudy.
Leave it alone, and it will become clear.
Let the stream flow, and it will find its way.
Stop chasing contentment, and it will come to you.

"MAYBE" and "perhaps" appear different,
But in reality are not,
Any more than ten thousand other fine distinctions,
Categories within categories,
Little boxes that hold nothing.
Why fear what others fear?
Why be misled by secondhand visions?
Leaders and followers are players in a game,
Moving in circles.

Others seem contented and amused,
Enjoying the feast,
Visiting the park,
Climbing the terrace in spring.
I appear aimless and alone—
A child who has not learned to smile.

Others have more wealth than they can manage;
I have nothing considered to be of value.
Others have immediate answers;
I do not even have clear questions.
Others rush to gain knowledge of the latest matters;
I appear ignorant and out of step,
Advised by the withdrawing tide,
Guided by the changing wind.

Others know more than I will ever know,
Have more than I will ever have,
Except for one thing.

BEFORE heaven and earth were known,
In the silent center of the whirling winds of change,
Something invisible appeared.
Without motion,
It produced unceasing activity.
Without voice,
It created countless sounds.
Without form,
It gave birth to ten thousand things.

It is timeless and immediate,
The door within the darkness,
The path to understanding.
It has no name;

Call it Tao,
The Way to Life.

Like a river,
It flows beyond vision.
Like a river,
It remains ever present.

The wise work with the ways of the earth.
The earth works with the ways of heaven.
Heaven works with the Way.

Tao works with what is natural.

WHEN a master gardener shapes a tree,
It seems to change without assistance;
No obvious cuts can be seen.
When a master carpenter joins wood,
Two pieces become one;
No gaps are visible.

A good speaker does not make one think of oratory;
A good writer does not draw attention to his words.
A good swimmer makes few ripples;
A good walker leaves no tracks.

The highest skill is hardly noticed,
Because it shows no trace of effort.
So it is with Tao.

When you find the Tao,
Others will find you.
Passing by on the road,
They will be drawn to your door.
The Tao that cannot be heard will be echoed in your voice.
The Tao that cannot be seen will be reflected in your eyes.
Though they may not know the source,
They will recognize happiness and peace.

Sweet music and highly seasoned food
Entertain for a while,
But the clear, tasteless water from the well
Gives life and energy without exhaustion.

FROM the action of opposites
Comes the order of the ten thousand things.

To lift a heavy object,
First push down on it.
To fill a container,
First empty it.
To have something return to you,
First let it go.
To receive,
First give.
To become wise,
First be a fool.

Gentleness is not weak,
Forcefulness is not strong.
Break attachment to halves,
And you will be whole.

FROM TAO came unity.
From this one thing came the dark and the light.
From these two things came energy, form, and substance.
From these three things came ten thousand more.
The ten thousand form the three,
The three form the two,
The two form the one.

If you destroy unity,
You destroy yourself.

WITH rulers,
The worst are hated,
The bad are feared,
The good are praised,
The best are not noticed.

A great leader takes no credit for his work.
When his actions are successful,
His followers celebrate their victory.

When those in power do not follow Tao,
The people do not follow them.

FORGET knowledge,
And you will remember all you need to know.
Forget sainthood,
And others will be remembered and helped.
Forget the rules of duty and respect,
And you will remember how to love.
Forget locks and guarded vaults,
And you will remember security and happiness.

Let others burden themselves
With the weight of unnecessary things;
Notice how they struggle as time goes by.
Become concerned with complexity,
And you will lose sight of simplicity.
You will have too much to remember,
And too much to forget.

THE HARSHEST storm
Can continue for only a little while.
If the power of heaven and earth
Cannot make such activity last for long,
How can you?

To find Tao,
Follow Tao.
To find truth,
Live the truth.
To find peace,
Learn to lose.

A violent man
Will not die peacefully.

THAT which has weight supports that which has little weight.
That which is calm sustains that which rushes around.
The unmoving leg of the compass makes the perfect circle possible.
The entire world works this way.

On a journey through unknown territory,
If you lose track of your food and supplies,
You will soon be unable to move.
The leader of an army of thousands knows this;
So does the man of Tao,
Moving through stability,
Rising through gravity.

WITHOUT traveling to foreign lands,
You can learn the way the world is made.
Without stepping on the stars,
You can see how they are arranged.
The farther you go in search of an answer,
The less you will understand.

Stop leaving,
And you will arrive.
Stop searching,
And you will see.
Stop running away,
And you will be found.

ALONG the way to knowledge,
Many things are accumulated.
Along the way to wisdom,
Many things are discarded.
Less and less effort is used,
Until things arrange themselves.

Harmonious action maintains control;
Exertion upsets the balance.

DEVELOP a man's strength,
But learn a woman's gentleness.
Attract without struggle;
Become a river of the world.
Like the river,
Return to the source.
Leave your egotistical ideas behind;
Become a child again.

Understand the energy of light,
But know the protection of the shadow.
Teach the truth by living;
Become a mirror of the ways of heaven.
As the mirror shines,
Reflecting light as well as darkness,
Show that life depends on both.

Achieve the highest,
But appear the lowest.
Attain humility;
Become the valley of the universe.
All things are brought to the valley;
All things come to those who open themselves.

When material is shaped to fulfill a narrow
function,
It can be used as a tool.
Build the foundation for independence;
Become the uncarved block.

THE WORLD is continually changing,
Yet constantly perfect;
It cannot be improved with your small efforts.
With larger efforts,
It can be destroyed.

The earth is a sacred vessel
Of spider webs and the wings of butterflies.
If you try to use it,
You will crush it.
If you try to change it,
It will shatter.
If you let it go,
It will remain useful.
If you leave it alone,
It will change for you.
Try to possess it,
And it will slip from your grasp.

Force yourself ahead,
And you will later be left behind.
Take more than your share,
And you will later have less than enough.
Overexert yourself,
And you will later become weak.

Too hard, you are easily pushed over;
Too soft, you cannot stand.

MANY say that following Tao
Is the way of a fool.
If it were not the way of a fool,
It would not be so simple.
If it were the way of the learned,
It would have vanished long ago,
Buried under rules and definitions.

Those known as fools may lack knowledge,
But knowledge is not wisdom.
Even the ignorant can understand this,
Yet those of learning do not.

Followers of Tao have three treasures:
To care,
To live moderately,
To value humility.

If you care, you will be unafraid.
If you live moderately, you will always have enough.
If you value humility, you can grow,
And become greater than you are.

Many try to be bold without caring,
To own riches without moderation,
To have greatness without humility.
They are on the way to death.

Those who care will be cared for.

THE WAY is so simple that complicated minds cannot see it;
Since they know so much, they know too little.
Because the Tao is constant and eternal, it is ignored;
If it were only a passing style, many would immediately try it.

The easily manipulated admire strange words and odd behavior;
The secret of the Tao is found in the smallest detail of the ordinary day.
Worthless glitter is quickly seen;
The most valuable jade is noticed last.

RESISTANCE follows force.
Thorns and weeds follow a passing army.
Years of misery follow victory in battle.
Struggling against Tao
Produces unnecessary loss of energy.

If you gain something and then brag about it,
You will not have it very long.

WEAPONS are instruments of evil;
Followers of Tao avoid them.
Those who value peace
Do not honor killing.
Those who do, oppose the laws
Of heaven, earth, and man.
Weapons are instruments of fear;
The great-hearted do not use them.

When many men are killed in battle,
Who can speak of celebration?
Destroying life is cause for sadness.
Conduct your victory like a funeral.

TAO is essentially simple,
But because it is unlimited,
It cannot be captured.
If rulers could make use of it,
Ten thousand things would be under their
command.
Heaven and earth would work for them,
As easily as rain falls from a cloudy sky.
The use of force would be forgotten;
Everything could take its natural place.

The unchanging center cannot be defined.
When its actions are seen,
They are given names,
Divisions are made,
And understanding becomes fragmented.
When the labels are removed,
What is underneath regains its dignity.

Tao contains the nameless and the named,
The formless and the formed,
Just as all the streams and rivers
Flow into the sea.

WATER is the softest thing on earth,
Yet its silken gentleness
Will easily wear away the hardest stone.
Everyone knows this;
Few use it in their daily lives.
Those of Tao yield and overcome.

To show fitness for ruling others,
Take their welfare upon your shoulders.
To have the strength to guide others,
Practice carrying their difficulties on your back.
Accept responsibility,
And power will be given to you.

Taller trees grow from lower ground.

THE REAL is not glamorous;
Glamor is not real.
Honesty does not persuade;
Persuasions are not honest.
Wisdom knows what cannot be told;
Foolishness tells without knowing.

The more you give away, the more you will gain.
When you discard the false, you will have room for the true.
Yield to others, and they will yield to you.
A sharp knife does not tear;
The Way to Life opens without effort.

UNDERSTANDING the outer is knowledge;
Understanding the inner is wisdom.
Control of others shows influence;
Control of the self reveals mastery.
Effort acquires possessions;
Contentment produces wealth.

Behind the order of the ten thousand things
Is no age,
No death.

THE TAO flows everywhere,
Creating,
Inspecting,
Remaining silent and unknown.
It rejects nothing,
Possesses nothing,
Encourages but does not dominate.

Being quiet,
Uncritical,
Nonpossessive,
It does not sign its name.
It is hardly recognized by anyone.
It is too small to see.

Secretly,
Unconsciously,
Without resistance,
The ten thousand things return to it.
It is too large to understand.

WHEN a nation is governed with Tao,
Goodness is common,
Spontaneous,
Unaware of itself.

When the Tao fades from view,
Cleverness appears.
When cleverness declines,
Ritual is formed.
When ritual is neglected,
Regulations arise.
When regulations deteriorate,
Force begins.

From force comes disorder and death.

THE GENTLEST force will conquer the most resisting force;
It is only a matter of time.
That which has no density can pass through limitations;
It is only a matter of space.
Time and space work with those who work with Tao.

Those who can teach without words
Will not be disputed with
By those who hear only words.
Those who can achieve without effort
Will not be opposed
By those who see only effort.

The wise become silent and invisible.
Being silent and invisible,
They are not interfered with.

YOUR NAME or your self—which is of more value to you?
Your possessions or your life—which will be harder to replace?

Become attached to fame,
And you will soon be separated from your true identity.
Gain too many things,
And you will lose awareness of your own existence.
Which way will you choose?

Difficult choices are easily made in matters of life or death.
Today is a matter of life or death.
There are many ways to die;
There is only one way to live.
Knowing when to stop will help you to begin.

WHEN the people work with Tao,
Horses haul fertilizer through the fields,
And there is food.

When the people work against Tao,
Horses are trained for war,
And there is starvation.

Those who take everything for themselves
Give trouble to everyone.
Those who envy the fortunes of others
Create misfortune for themselves.
Those who develop their original wealth
Bring riches wherever they go.

THE WAY is easy,
But crooked paths are popular.

When the fields are exhausted
And the granaries are empty,
The palaces are full
And the occupants fat and lazy.
Their fine clothes and sharp swords
Only emphasize the fact
That they are robbers.

What is sensible behavior?
Walk the main road;
Avoid danger.

HE WHO has Tao has no fear,
Causes no harm,
Displays no strength.
Since he has no fear within him,
Those who feed on fear are not attracted to him.
Since he causes no harm,
No harm can return to him.
Since he displays no strength,
No one can estimate his power.

Achieve balance,
And you will achieve anything.
Rush to accomplish something,
And you will upset the plan.
Hold your breath,
And you will be forced to gasp for air.
Use too much energy,
And you will reach exhaustion,
But will miss the Tao.

Whatever works against natural laws will not
last long.

LAWS may govern a state,
Strategies may win wars,
But empires are kept alive the longest
By doing what is required to rule,
And no more.

How can we know this is true?

Taxes are passed,
"To benefit the people."
The more taxes there are,
The more poverty increases.

Weapons are accumulated,
"To protect the people."
The more weapons there are,
The more threats and danger.

Clever officials are appointed,
"To serve the people."
The more clever they are,
The more confusion rules the land.

Regulations are written,
"To guide the people."
The more regulations,
The more robbery and lying.

Without taxes,
There is wealth.
Without weapons,
There is peace.
Without cleverness,
There is order.
Without regulations,
There is honesty.

As interfering help is given,
Ability and confidence are taken away.

THROUGHOUT the universe,
No treasure can compare with Tao.
It provides help and encouragement to those of moral strength,
And gives those trapped by evil a chance to free themselves.

Good words win honor in the eyes of men,
But good deeds win the Tao.
Abandoning the misguided without helping them to change their fate
Will take you far from the Tao.

On the day the emperor is crowned,
And the officers of state installed,
When others hurry forward with gifts of jade and dancing horses,
Remain behind and send the Tao.

DARKNESS starts with a shadow;
Great confusion develops from a little disorder.

A tree as wide as a man can reach begins with a small seed.
A terrace one hundred feet high begins with a shovelful of earth.
A journey of a thousand miles begins with a single step.

Whether something is successful or tragic
Depends upon how it ends.
Everyone knows this.
How something will end
Can be determined by how it begins.
Very few know this.
If attention is given to the beginning,
There will be no tragedy.
If care is given to the ending,
There will be no failure.

If you want to achieve greatness,
You will need to master the small deeds that it is made of.
If you want to understand complexity,
You will need to see the simple things that it contains.

Then the great will be small,
The complex will be simple,
Effort will vanish,
And all things will arrange themselves in order.
The wise see no problem as big.

The wise see no problem as small.
They do not underestimate their responsibilities,
They are not misled by appearances,
They make no easy promises.

Those who underestimate their responsibilities
Overburden their abilities.
Those who are misled by appearances
Mislead others and make matters worse.
Those who make easy promises
Encounter difficulties.

WHICH is greater—passion or compassion?

It takes courage to face death;
It takes more courage to face life.
It takes strength to kill;
It takes more strength to protect.

This is simple and obvious,
But even the highest in the land have trouble seeing it.

Although you may not be able to forgive those who do wrong,

The ways of heaven are merciful.
Although you may wink your eye at those who cause evil,
The eyes of heaven never close.
The Tao of heaven does not speak,
Yet it responds;
Does not move,
Yet it is everywhere;
Does not call,
Yet everything returns to it in time.
Its net has wide meshes,
But nothing slips through.

THOSE who are unafraid to say they do not know
Become wise.
Those who insist they know
Never learn.

Those who pay attention to their weaknesses
Gain strength.
Those who neglect their strength
Become weak.

Wisdom and strength come from the courage
To see things as they are.

WHEN immature apprentices
Take a master craftsman's place,
Respect for merchandise declines;
Articles can be destroyed without regret.

When revengeful rulers
Take the universal governor's place,
Respect for life declines;
Execution of criminals has no effect.

If people do not value life,
How can they be controlled
With threats of death?
Use the master's knife,
And sooner or later,
You will cut yourself.

INFLEXIBLE fighters lose in battle;
Unbending trees fall in the storm.
Life grows and changes;
Death remains rigid.

When a plant is dead at its center,
It resists the wind
And is easily broken in two.
Hard,
Demanding,
Dead in your heart,
You invite the natural forces
To finish the process.
Proud,
Unyielding,
Dead in your mind,
You will be snapped
When the wind changes direction.

TAO MOVES by returning,
Overcomes by attracting.
This gives its actions weight and power;
No force can last against them.

Movement from stillness,
Existence from emptiness—
From absolute Nothing
Comes everything.

WHEN shown the Way,
The strong watch and work with it,
The weak think about it,
The nearsighted laugh at it.
Whenever it is laughed at,
It becomes "mysterious" and "dark."

To those who have trouble seeing,
The easy appears to be difficult,
Simplicity appears to be complex,
Wisdom appears to be foolish,
Endurance appears to be weak,
Great accomplishments appear to be small,
Real beauty appears to be plain,
The temporary appears to be eternal.

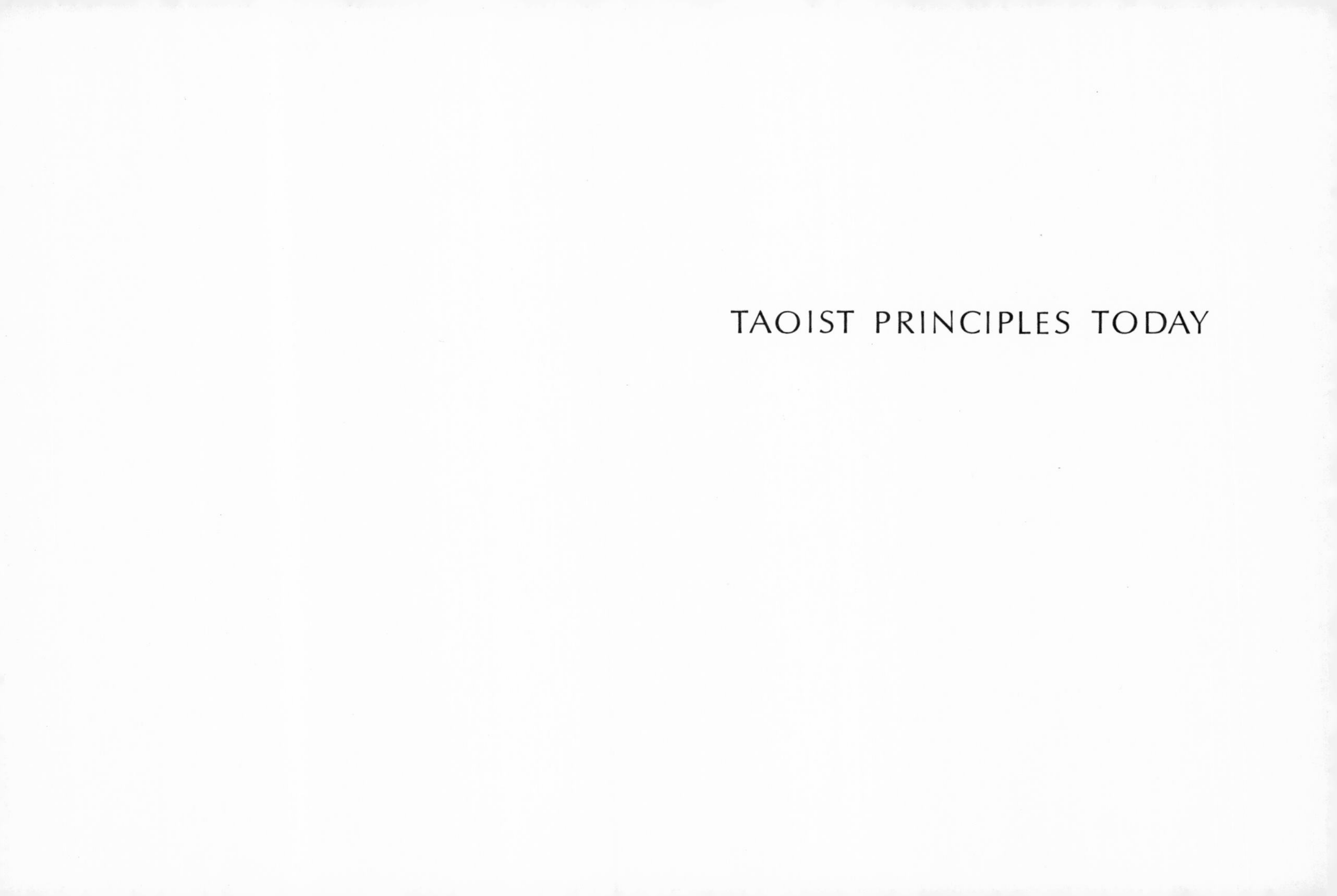

TAOIST PRINCIPLES TODAY

THE SOURCE

Like the river,
Return to the source.

In many places pools of water can be seen, fed by springs hidden deep within the ground. Some are clean, some contaminated, but in the center of each, clear water bubbles and splashes upward from its source. In a similar way every unhappy human spirit has the power to restore itself. But in either case poisoning from the outside must first be stopped.

The five colors blind the eye.
The five sounds deafen the ear.
The five flavors deaden the appetite.
Chasing and killing destroy the heart.
Precious possessions cripple one's mastery;
They end up owning their owners.

Drugged and distracted by endless diversions, many are out of touch with the source. There are those who believe that inner happiness in life can somehow come from the accumulation of lifeless external matter. Lacking confidence in their own undeveloped abilities, the possession-hungry are easily persuaded that they can be considered young, attractive, clever, and lovable if they only buy the latest thing. But the latest thing begins to age as soon as it is acquired, decreasing the value of its purchasers and turning them into used things to be used by others. In the unsatisfying struggle to buy artificial importance in the form of transient metal and plastic trinkets, the eternal treasure of happiness is overlooked.

Many seem to believe that they will find happiness by losing themselves in a powerful industry's expensive efforts to turn the destruction of human morality, civilized values, and even life itself into profit-making entertainment. Like the village idiot who eats from trash cans and then wonders why he feels weaker than before, the commercially convinced buyer of bestiality feeds his subconscious mind with socially and spiritually contaminating garbage, and is then unable to understand why coldness, cruelty, and criminal conduct are increasing around him, and why a vague emotional numbness is spreading within. Poisoning his own mind and spirit, subjecting his miraculously sensitive nervous and glandular systems to unnaturally high levels of stressful stimulation, and contributing his money to mercenary sensation salesmen for the privilege of being pushed and pulled around like a small pawn on a giant chessboard, he is led to believe that he is somehow escaping from, rather than adding to, his problems. But the problems become greater for all. No individual can find a strong foundation for future survival in a society that supports the assassination of life values as popular amusement. Trouble is naturally attracted to the negative magnetism that radiates unconsciously from minds conditioned to ignore the most basic moral distinctions. In the search for ever-increasing sensations along the road of sickness and death, the commercially manipulated miss the way to happiness and health.

Many others believe that happiness is to be found through the immediate gratification of obsessive appetites, appetites that are never satisfied but that increase with each feeding. A great number believe that they will gain personal happiness by attaching themselves to other people as emotional parasites, but no one can share the happiness of love with them because they do not develop the source of love within themselves and therefore have nothing to give.

Others believe that happiness can be built up in endless cycles of compulsive physical activity, or attained through the equally exhausting pursuit of abstract goals, titles, or positions. Never having relaxed with themselves long enough to have known what happiness is, they do not quite know what to look for. Yet they relentlessly run after what appears to be its elusive shadow, feeling certain that they will catch up with it on the last step of the stairway or around the next corner as they chase away their limited time on earth.

A pathetically large number believe that they can anesthetize themselves into a state of happiness with reality-distorting substances that in time produce clouded senses, lowered energy levels, timid, conformist behavior, emotional and nutritional deficiencies, premature aging, low-quality work, and illusions of creativity and power. Not realizing that the spirit can accomplish nothing of importance in this world without a functioning physical vehicle, these pacifier-dependents damage and destroy the irreplaceable instruments of their own minds and bodies for a few brief moments of artificial energy and irrelevant insights that they are spiritually unprepared for and emotionally unequipped to handle and that cause no actual improvements in their everyday activities.

Still others search for happiness by listening to strange voices from the outer darkness, or by attending expensive weekend workshops where they are sold methods of "finding" themselves, within the right groups, or by joining instant religions centered around obsessed leaders with strangely unreligious desires for ever-increasing amounts of money and political power.

All of these people are afraid of themselves. They miss the source of lasting happiness because it is found in the one place they never look—within themselves. It has been there from the beginning, an endless supply of understanding, happiness, and peace.

> When you discard the false,
> You will have room for the true.

The Chinese character for wisdom (*hui*) shows a broom held over the mind-heart. The basic truth it represents was obvious to the ancient masters who formed it, and is every bit as meaningful today. When the contaminating effects of external influence have been cleared away through meditation and related disciplines, the source will eventually be felt reflected within, like an unmoving mirror image of the power constantly active in the outer world. No language can describe its atmosphere, like soundless singing and silent laughter. Once found, it will never be forgotten, and imitations will sooner or later be left behind.

THE UNCARVED BLOCK

> Along the way to knowledge,
> Many things are accumulated.
> Along the way to wisdom,
> Many things are discarded.

Through daily contact with the source, harmful habits acquired through years of indoctrination and persuasion, as well as the labels and uniforms of external identities, can slowly be removed, leaving the simplicity of the original self. The formless, creative source of unity will then be reflected in a clear, constructive mind. Taoists refer to this state as the uncarved block (*p'u*), described in chapters 20 and 28 of the *Tao Te Ching*. The unperceptive often mistake its unaffected character for ignorance or lack of intelligence, not recognizing it as an essential element of practical genius.

> Leave your egotistical ideas behind;
> Become a child again.

Those of the uncarved block are not affected by flattering remarks and favorable opinions, or afraid of seeming to be fools. Since they have mastered ego, there is no struggle in their lives. Skills seem to develop without effort, opposition is easily overcome. With clear and independent minds, they are able to react quickly and spontaneously to dangerous or changing situations. Working with the laws of heaven and earth, they recognize meaning and value within what others see as only accidents and coincidence, and see through the ghosts known as bad luck and good fortune.

THE SPIRIT OF THE VALLEY

> The Spirit of the Valley
> Creates life without end.

At the center of all noncombative, nonegotistical action is an aspect of Tao personified as the Spirit of the Valley, a mysterious stillness, seen as feminine in character, from which wisdom, strength, and skillful activity are born. This can be felt within when the mind has reached what Chinese Taoists refer to as *hsu chi ching tu*—absolute emptiness, complete quiet. Sitting in late-night meditation, one becomes well acquainted with the Spirit of the Valley.

> All things are brought to the valley;
> All things come to those who open themselves.

As a vacuum draws in that which is outside of it, as a river collects that which flows from above it, and as a valley is filled by that which is around it, so a nonegotistical mind attracts what it needs without struggle. Because the aggressive exertion of egotistical pursuit is dense and deliberate, it appears powerful. But it can be laughed at when the superior strength of attraction is attained.

Whatever works
against natural laws
will not last long.

In reality, the principles of Tao are as much in operation here at this moment as they were 4,500 years ago in China at the time of the first recorded Taoist, the legendary Yellow Emperor. Still, many overanalytical minds regard them only as philosophical ideas and fail to understand the importance of these governing forces in action. Others ignore the rules completely and create situations that ultimately lead to disaster.

At the present time, we move about on technological crutches that temporarily allow the dangerous illusion that we can now afford to interrupt the eternal flow of universal laws. A conscious connection with the real world is being severed, and its absence is conspicuous in a morally, spiritually, and sexually lost society resembling an elaborate sailing vessel cut adrift without a rudder. In waging mechanical warfare against the living earth, our only home, many who call themselves modern are obviously out of touch with today and separated from their surroundings as well. In action, they resemble retarded children playing with matches in a wooden barn. With confused, impatient minds, they mistake blind movement in the wrong direction for progress, yet at the same time stubbornly persist in dangerously outdated approaches to living.

When members of other species are being exterminated by chemicals formulated to destroy the "pests" they feed upon, then putting more poisonous compounds into the world's food, air, and water to counter the inevitable attacks of increasingly chemically-immune creatures reveals a definite disturbance of the normal powers of reasoning.

When the human race gives itself the right to multiply to numbers far in excess of those that the earth can support beyond a few more years, and when the necessary balance provided by natural population controls has been nullified by science for "humanitarian" reasons, then producing babies in fertility-drugged women and laboratory test tubes, socially and financially encouraging couples to breed offspring, and congratulating those who bring more children into a world that does not want them and that will soon be unable to feed them could certainly be considered signs of unsound behavior.

When electrical energy is generated by creating radioactive poisons that remain deadly for thousands of years, then transporting them without warning through heavily populated areas and storing them in containers that last only a short time, while ignoring the tremendous natural power of the wind and sun, clearly indicates that contact with the world of reality has been lost.

> Less and less effort is used,
> Until things arrange themselves.

The Taoist term *wu wei* (no doing, no causing) indicates an attitude of working with, rather than against, natural laws. Misunderstood by many to mean taking no action, *wu wei* actually refers to taking whatever action is most effective and least disruptive for the immediate moment, just as a Taoist master of self-defense easily and calmly overcomes an attacker without even appearing to move. Those who practice *wu wei* work in harmony with the natural alternation of movement and rest found in the real world so that no action on their part is noticeable—everything seems to arrange itself, with a minimum amount of difficulty. Inflexibly doing nothing is unnatural and is therefore not *wu wei*. In practice, the term can be interpreted as no force, noninterference, or without struggle. More than any other, it represents the Taoist approach to living.

> Harmonious action maintains control;
> Exertion upsets the balance.

In reality, control of life has nothing to do with energy-draining rigidity or warlike struggle. Real life is constantly changing; real control calls for the power to move quickly when speed is required and the ability to wait when patience is necessary. Without inner stillness, such spontaneous response is impossible.

The Taoist believes that the world is normally in a state of perfect balance, as various forces counteract each other, obeying natural laws. Disturbances arise within the restless egotistical mind, causing combative actions that upset the ordinary equilibrium of the physical and social surroundings. Sooner or later they return, in one form or another, as everything eventually returns to its source. The misunderstanding mind does not recognize them, nor does it know what is behind their seemingly sudden appearance. It then attacks them as problems unconnected to its own greed—economics, politics, the environment—without doing anything to correct their cause. Such attitudes only allow the damage to increase. In this way the never-satisfied ego sets dangerous cycles in motion, damaging and destroying everything that matters.

TZ' U

From compassion comes greatness,
From greatness comes Tao.

In chapters 19 and 67 of the *Tao Te Ching, tz'u* is mentioned, Lao-tze's "first treasure." In written Chinese, it is composed of the radical *hsin,* heart, placed beneath *tzu,* luxuriant vegetation, indicating a fertile, unfolding heart. In English, it could be called caring. The Taoist believes that the rigidity of ego can best be worn away by the gentleness of caring, as mountains are worn away by the sea. The first treasure is the force that overcomes apathy, cruelty, and fear, as well as the key that opens the mind to understanding. *Tz'u* is the secret reason why the cold-hearted can be clever, but never wise—the superior man, the real man, is one who cares.

THE WAY

The road that can be measured
is not the endless road.

Whenever it is allowed and encouraged to, the restless intellect builds barriers of misunderstanding, cleverly isolating individuals from each other and skillfully separating them from their common source. Beyond these walls of the crafty but limited analytical mind lies a limitless eternal power. Looking out upon it are the windows of sectarian religions and philosophies, each allowing a finite glimpse of the infinite and indefinable, framed by doctrines, definitions, and differences—the materials that form the walls. As more and more distinctions are made, the openings become narrower and smaller.

Why fear what others fear?
Why be misled by secondhand visions?

As an example of useful understanding, how can you get to know the moon? You can ask those who analyze the dust particles and rocks brought back from its surface to tell you of its true nature. But when your head is filled with only surface knowledge, with dust and rocks, there will be no room within it for the moon. You can learn something about its character by asking anyone who watches it at night. But whatever information you may gain from someone else's observations will be from someone else's point of view and therefore limited in practical use. You can read many books about the moon, but since most of what they can tell you is not connected to your personal experience nor something you can apply to daily life, it will eventually be forgotten. If you really want to become acquainted with the moon, step outside and look at it.

If you walk along the beach at night, you can see the distant moon low on the horizon, drawing the waves away, or watch as it rises high above, pulling the tides to shore. When you see its effects in front of you and feel its magnetic strength within, you will start to understand it for yourself. So it is with the Way.

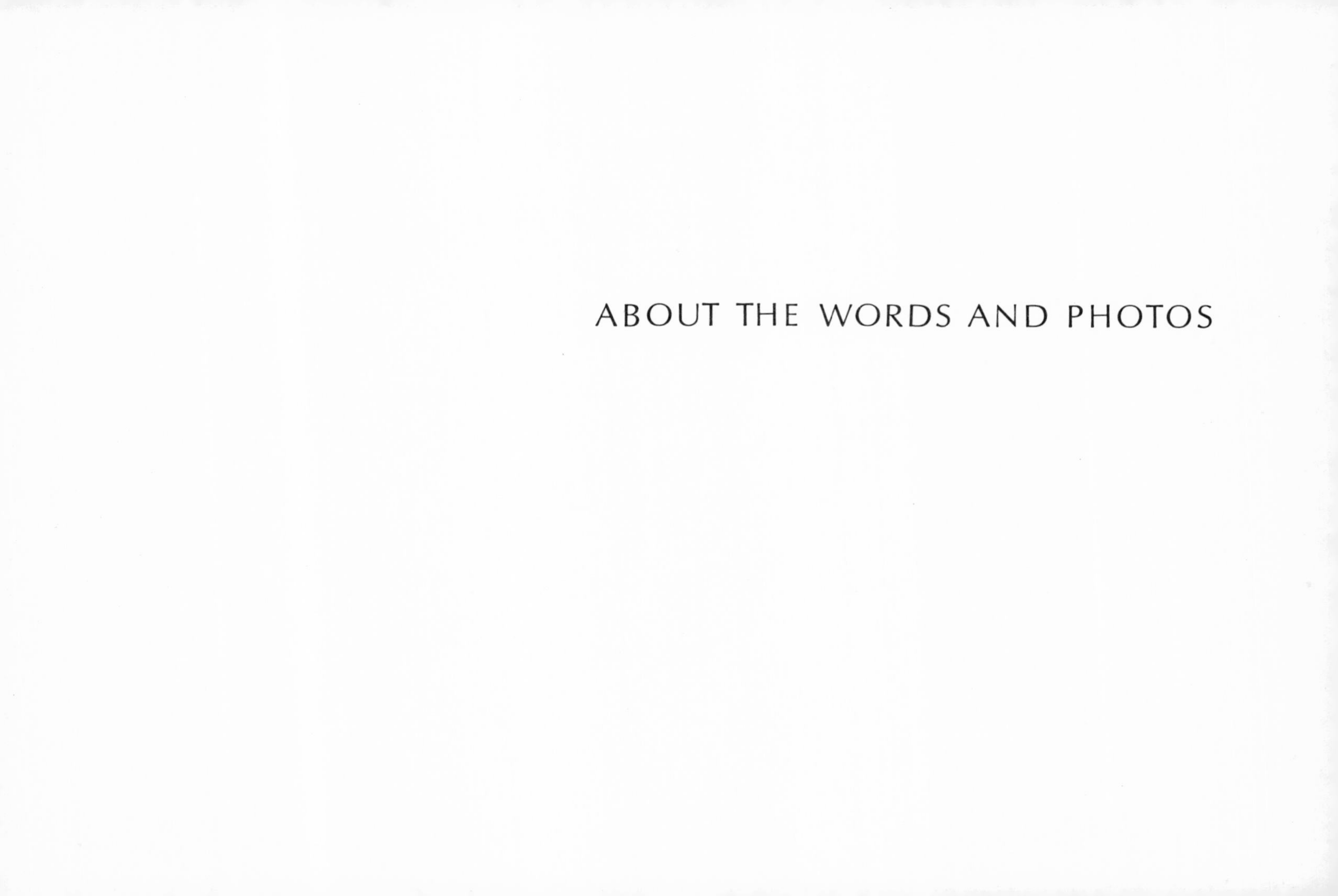

ABOUT THE WORDS AND PHOTOS

THE WORDS

Stir muddy water,
and it will stay cloudy.

There are many English-language versions of the *Tao Te Ching,* written by scholars far more knowledgeable than myself. Yet for my purposes, each seems to lack the simplicity, clarity, and unity of the Taoist "uncarved block." Rather than attempt to add one more translation from the professional point of view of the scholar, I chose to present one interpretation from the everyday practice of a Taoist. The chapters that seemed most representative and concise are used to describe the basic themes.

Why an interpretation? Although there are several ancient versions of the *Tao Te Ching* in existence, each is different. The original no longer exists. What are called translations are in reality interpretations, each based upon previous translations of translations. In the past, Chinese translators tended to switch verses around to suit their own expression, add comments of their own, and incorporate quotations from other sources into the body of the text. This tendency to modify was not limited to scholars. Until the Communists gained governmental control, children would learn sayings from the *Tao Te Ching* in school, often in the form of songs or verses, and all were encouraged to make up their own interpretations based upon their own understanding.

From the point of view of many modern scholars, therefore, the *Tao Te Ching* is a victim of centuries of amateurish intellectual tampering. But there is another point of view. Many of the changes made were improvements based upon perceptive understanding of the nature of the book, a masterpiece of mystical communication whose universal essence reaches out to us over an incredible distance in time and space. Those changes have kept the *Tao Te Ching* alive. "If it were the way of the learned," chapter 67 states, "it would have vanished long ago." The principles of the *Tao Te Ching* are its true language and are what needs to be expressed; the English words or Chinese characters only represent them. When latter-day scholars nearsightedly argue over translation differences and details, they are standing on what may appear to be solid ground, but which was in historic reality constantly shifting in order to best express the meanings to the people of the times. The dead atmosphere of many supposedly modern English-language versions is due at least in part to futile attempts to freeze the ever-flowing, ever-changing *Tao Te Ching* into rigid ice that can be neatly carved into little pieces by examiners of unimportant particulars.

> Leave it alone, and it will become clear.
> Let the stream flow, and it will find its way.

After reading the various translations of a chapter, I would close the books and clear my mind of all thoughts and words. In the stillness, the differences in interpretation would recede and the essential meanings appear. Then I would begin to write. Each chapter would be written and rewritten until it seemed complete.

THE PHOTOGRAPHS

> The secret of the Tao
> is found in the smallest detail
> of the ordinary day.

Following the Taoist principle of nonegotistical reflection, unmanipulated, full-frame photographs are used to illustrate various chapters. In agreement with the Taoist attitude of not searching "beyond your door," all were taken locally, at areas I am familiar with.

THE CAMERA AND THE MIND

> Become a mirror
> of the ways of heaven.

My photography equipment is very simple: an Olympus OM-1 with two lenses, a 50 mm macro and a 200 mm telephoto. I use ASA 64 Kodachrome exclusively. My method of working is also simple: I use as few frames of film as possible, I never crop or alter a print, I pay little attention to photography and photographers, and often when taking pictures, I am even unconscious of the camera in my hand. I watch the light reflected from objects, mentally seeing it on the film, and only use the camera when the lighting is exactly right. Then I tend to move very fast. I carry a tripod but rarely use it, preferring the speed and flexibility of hand-held photography. Sunlight can make subtle changes very quickly and even a strong wind will pause for a fraction of a second. Whether I capture or miss the image at such a moment, I put it out of my mind with the click of the shutter—otherwise the next opportunity will be affected.

Aside from a few classes in photography, I have learned photography mostly on my own, often practicing without film in order to minimize attachment and encourage a "mirror-mind." Most of my training in composition and color sense has been in the areas of drawing and painting. But the mind-clearing practices taught me by masters of the Chinese martial arts have been the strongest influence.

In both photography and self-defense, a method must be relentlessly practiced, step by step, until it can be used without thinking, for in actual application there is often no time to think. An undisciplined mind cannot accomplish this; neither can a mind that concerns itself with details at the expense of principles. As in the martial arts, a mind that understands the principles can create its own tactics and gain control of a situation, while a lazy, ignorant, or cluttered mind will remain at the mercy of circumstances. In either area, a real mastery of techniques depends upon a mastery of the mind. The camera is not as important as the eye, and the eye is useless without the mind.

Revealing the nature of Tao through the medium of photography requires undistorted reflection of its outer actions and appearances as well as transmission of its inner character of stillness. Photographs that show one side alone cannot indicate the wholeness of Tao. Since something is missing from them, they decrease in value with each examination.

Watching as things arrange themselves in the changing light, the photographer with unobstructed vision sees them as they are. Appropriate images appear without struggle, moving with the flow of light like leaves in a stream, to be immediately reflected in a mind unclouded by preconceived ideas. It may be necessary to proceed slowly and cautiously or to move at great speed. In either case, no wandering, egotistical thoughts can be allowed to interfere. If the mind is quiet and concentrated, the actions instinctive, the photographer can pass through the world noticing but unnoticed, like a cat slipping silently through the sunlight and shadows.

FINDING LIST

The chapter numbers shown below are those traditionally used in the *Tao Te Ching*. The page numbers refer to the present book, followed by numbers in parentheses to indicate whether a selection appears on the (1) left or (2) right side of a given page.

FROM TRANSLATIONS TO ORIGINALS

page	chapter
13	1
14	5
15 (1)	6
15 (2)	12
16	7
19	8
20	16
23	18
24 (1)	11
24 (2)	13
25	15
26	20
29	25
30	27
33	35
34	36
37	42
38 (1)	17
38 (2)	19
39 (1)	23
39 (2)	26
40	47
43	48
44	28
45	29
46	67
49	70
50 (1)	30
50 (2)	31
51	32
52	78
55	81
56 (1)	33
56 (2)	34
57 (1)	38
57 (2)	43
58	44
59 (1)	46
59 (2)	53
60	55
61	57
62 (1)	62
62 (2)	64
63	63
64	73
65 (1)	71
65 (2)	74
66 (1)	76
66 (2)	40
67	41

FROM ORIGINALS TO TRANSLATIONS

chapter	page	chapter	page	chapter	page	chapter	page
1	13	20	26	36	34	57	61
5	14	23	39 (1)	38	57 (1)	62	62 (1)
6	15 (1)	25	29	40	66 (2)	63	63
7	16	26	39 (2)	41	67	64	62 (2)
8	19	27	30	42	37	67	46
11	24 (1)	28	44	43	57 (2)	70	49
12	15 (2)	29	45	44	58	71	65 (1)
13	24 (2)	30	50 (1)	46	59 (1)	73	64
15	25	31	50 (2)	47	40	74	65 (2)
16	20	32	51	48	43	76	66 (1)
17	38 (1)	33	56 (1)	53	59 (2)	78	52
18	23	34	56 (2)	55	60	81	55
19	38 (2)	35	33				

The "weathermark" identifies this book as a production of John Weatherhill, Inc., publishers of fine books on Asia and the Pacific. Book design and typography by Meredith Weatherby and Margaret Taylor. Composition by Samhwa, Seoul. Printing of the text and engraving and printing of the plates, in four-color offset, by Kinmei, Tokyo. Binding by Makoto Binderies, Tokyo. The text is set in 12- and 14-point Monotype Bembo, with hand-set Optima for display.